REACH FOR THE COOKIES

METAPHYSICALLY FLAVORED APHORISMS AND ILLUSTRATIONS

By Dick Jachim

CES PUBLISHING
P.O. Box 55967
Sherman Oaks, CA 91403

Paperback edition of
"Reach For The Cookies"

First published in 1987
by CES PUBLISHING.

All Rights Reserved.

Printed in the U.S.A.
Copyright pending.

ISBN: 0-940469-00-6

COVER BY: Dick Jachim and Doriane Lee Parker.

Dedicated to practitioners of the Science Of Mind discipline.

ACKNOWLEDGEMENTS

In reflection, on completing this book, the conclusion is that a book is the composition of encouragement, faith, and guidance from others and then of the author's creation. For this reason, names of appreciation must be mentioned. Those left out unintentionally I must reckon with as they come to mind.

Rev. Virginia Saville, from the United Church of Religious Science, Seattle, Washington. She was an encouragement throughout and used the illustrations which were sent to her as teaching tools in her metaphysical classes.

Patricia A. and James R. Murphy, Directors of The Arizona Health Care Research Institute, Inc. They utilize the illustrations by bringing them to the attention of their clients to help create an attitude conducive to healing.

Les Kaufman, publicist for forty-five years in the motion picture industry; many of those years were with Don Fedderson Productions and Lawrence Welk before retiring. As a student of metaphysics, he enthusiastically encouraged this book because it is a refreshing respite when spirits are low.

The members of the Board of the League of Religious Science Practitioners for publicizing the book before its completion at their spring and fall conferences. Unable to name all the members; by mentioning, however, Vivain Thezan and Phyllis English should prove a good representation.

I bless the Sorensens, Stephanie and Rev. Christian from the Ventura Church of Religious Science and Revs. Paul and Jackie from the Newhall Church for their continuous encouragement.

An assist is also attributed to Grace Wittenberger who is known for her channeling of: Teachings From Expanded Mental Dimensions, under the title of *Cosmic Energy and Man Aligned,* for appraising segments of the book as it was being written.

And lastly, because it was the place where it all began, the North Hollywood Church of Religious Science, where Dr. Carlo Di Giovanna is the Minister. By the placement of metaphysically flavored cartoons in the church newsletter, the idea for this book was born.

Table of Contents

CHAPTER ONE
Welcome into the Parlour of my Mind 11

CHAPTER TWO
Begins with Abundance and ends with Balance 15

CHAPTER THREE
Can Fear be an Ally is highlighted 29

CHAPTER FOUR
Goal of Life – to Judgmental 51

CHAPTER FIVE
Level of Acceptance – to Love 69

CHAPTER SIX
Personality – to Success 91

CHAPTER SEVEN
Thought – to The Undisciplined Word 107

Chapter 1

Welcome into the Parlour of my Mind

The original idea was to create a book of cartoons and foot notes with a metaphysical flavor. This thought expanded along the way to add a page of short remarks or aphorisms, for each illustration. This was inspired after a very qualified teacher of the "Science of Mind" philosophy mentioned that she used some of the illustrations as teaching tools. Grateful for this information, it then occurred that the illustrations and aphorisms should be alphabetically categorized in the Table of Contents. This allows them to be easily found as a frame of reference, especially since many overlap to some degree. Going down the line of the alphabet, each chapter has its own group.

Chapter 2 begins with abundance, and includes two illustrations with different approaches. One, not to look for abundance but to accept it and, secondly, through the law of circulation. The next two illustrations are about attitude depicted by twins and then about how you cannot escape your attitudes. Following is about balance with two illustrations; one shows weight evenly distributed by luggage in each hand, and the other with the value of books.

Going on to Chapter 3, ego with three illustrations is on top of the list. One of them refers to the bloated-self, followed by virtue as vice, and to laughing at oneself for number three. Enthusiasm is the next, showing obstacles overcome handily; next the illustration of faith, showing courage even at the level of a worm. False Gods, which is an illustration of ugly faces, follows.

Continuing with Chapter 3, there are two illustrations about fear. Fear is undoubtedly the most prevalent and distressing emotion known; enough deterrents cannot be offered to neutralize it. Each illustration is dramatically convincing of the power of fear. The first by showing a human head hidden in sand with an ostrich looking on, and the second with an elephant's fear hallucinating an enormous shadow of an enemy, the mouse. Fear is seldom, if ever, expressed as an ally, yet there are circumstances where it seems to be so. There was an experience during World War II when I was a medic in a combat unit, the Second Armored Division, a tank division, which fought through North Africa and Sicily, then to England for the invasion of France. We went on to be the first American Troops in Belgium, then through to Holland and on to the Siegfred Line, the German bordered fortress; and completing the tour as the first American Troops in Berlin. This success could not have been accomplished without first compromising fear. It was quickly realized in combat that fear causes adrenaline to flow freely. This activates one's alertness and ability to a fine edge of readiness. This creates an intense presence of mind, which offers a greater chance for survival. Though a harsh lesson, it changes the attitude towards fear from an adversary to a condoned ally. On a smaller scale, this compares with teaching swimming by pushing the student into the deep end of the pool. Fear alerts survival and the student thrashes to safety, and improves the thrashing into swimming with each experience.

The next illustration dwells on feeling inadequate; here a turkey feels persecuted. This chapter ends with forgiveness, which, when sincere becomes a pass to the theatre of life.

Chapter 4 begins with two illustrations on the goal of life. One shows encouragement to hang in there at all costs, and the second focuses on the level of happiness desired. The next shows that to improve yourself is to improve the universe. An illustration on insight is next; a water scene with an in-depth discussion between a fish and a duck. Irritation is next, which sometimes is beneficial as shown in this instance. Jealousy becomes a toad, and then two illustrations on being judgmental follow. One is about attraction and the other, a superior attitude gives an opinion.

Chapter 5 has level of acceptance showing three shoppers with their purchases. Next, limitation is represented in two ways; confusion is highlighted in one and warped thoughts in the form of a fence in the other. Life in limitless variations depicts a scene of the world; then six illustrations on love are next; beginning with a dog's loyalty, followed by tolerance, then loving oneself. Love is next reflected in the beauty found in flowers, then young love sparkling everywhere, and finishing with the love found in a hug.

Chapter 6 finds personality illustrated in three ways. One is about a doughnut, another compliments an egg and the third shows a group of smiling faces. A cat with a mouse as the prop reflects poise next. Two illustrations represent a problem; one shows a problem as an opportunity, and how a mistake can be beneficial in the other. Scaling poles is the final illustration in this chapter, depicting success.

Chapter 7 starts with six illustrations on thought. They are from an air balloon, to domesticating habits, followed by negativities melting away; a scene of poverty and riches is next, and then an empty vessel, and closing with a welcomed greeting through an open door. Tranquility is next shown in two ways. Both depict effortless effort in a comfortable way. This chapter, and the book, ends with an illustration on the undisciplined word; a ball and chain around the neck of a dreary figure, and another figure seated, relaxed and composed. Guess which of the two speaks the undisciplined word?

Chapter 2

Abundance is a creative form in the universe awaiting acceptance.

The quantity of substance available, however, is determined not by desire, which usually is a cosmetic thought, but by the mental level of acceptance.

To attract more abundance, will first necessitate becoming more; that is, growing in consciousness.

That is why everybody is in their right place at the present time, at capacity.

**DON'T LOOK FOR ABUNDANCE.
JUST ACCEPT IT.**

Practicing the Law of Circulation is the manifestation of the thought initiated returning many fold.

In this case the affirmative willingness on the part of the parent of the bride to readily and generously distribute the necessary funds, time and space for a successful wedding assures abundance to return many fold to the giver.

In addition, the many treasures of happiness experienced, by this action, are safely tucked away in memory already.

Thought of prosperity attracts prosperity.

AS THE WEDDING ENDS, THE LAW OF CIRCULATION BEGINS FOR THE FATHER OF THE BRIDE. HURRY LAW!

The pattern for living can be ageless if activities continue to be exhilarating to the pattern maker.

The physical tempo may become moderated, but the enthusiasm for being active continues to be intense.

This combination finds contemporary life readily acceptable, and it is reflected in the attitude.

Mellowing with age where the calendar is featured, is also a pattern for living, but is so time consuming.

ONE TWIN MEASURES AGE BY THE CALENDAR. THE OTHER BY ATTITUDE.

Attitudes flavored with love, tolerance, humor, and charity live in a free, joyous world.

Those accented with severity, limitation, unforgiveness and that are opinionated know a world of severe restrictions with continuous striving for survival.

Pick the attitudes and the world comes with them.

All are exchangeable.

YOU CANNOT ESCAPE YOUR ATTITUDES, BUT YOU CAN CHANGE THEM.

Being in balance with the universe is an attitude that focuses on wholeness, as being one with God.

This attunement with the Divine Expression is to know that fullness in health, happiness and prosperity prevails.

It is the practice of living effortlessly. To maintain this attitude, if effort seeps in, stop and refocus from within and return thoughts ahead, again, to the effortless effort level, the balance with the universe.

IN BALANCE, STRENGTH MULTIPLIES AND EFFORT DIMINISHES.

A book! The highly respected communicator of the universe.

It is the willing companion in any interest, no matter how diversified it may be.

It can be a comic, a poet, a scientist or even a mystery.

It can raise the consciousness or the body when a bit more height is needed.

Here is a friend versatile, and especially, so dependable that it is uplifting.

BOOKS ARE UPLIFTING.

р
Chapter 3

When the image insists on the center stage for every performance in the drama of life, the personality can be victimized into a false reality of hero worshipping of oneself.

Unchecked, this self-importance grows into a *bloated-self*. Larger and larger with every performance. Eventually obscuring the light of life.

Pushing it aside, our hero finds true salvation in the form of a balanced life and lives happily ever after.

SOMETIMES IT IS NECESSARY TO PUSH ASIDE THE BLOATED-SELF TO SEE THE LIGHT FOR ONE'S GOOD.

Virtue that flows from within is inherent with truth and moral qualities. It refines the sense of love and beauty, as well as the concept of life.

The end result is the flow in harmony with the universe in all endeavors.

Virtue conscious of itself is an intellectual dialogue created for a desired affect to serve only a given purpose for personal gain.

Such a compromise is limited in substance and distorts virtue and turns it into vice.

VIRTUE CONSCIOUS OF ITSELF IS VICE.

Laughing at oneself is an affront to artificial grandeur, to the point that desertion may take place.

This then can activate a severe personality change, to where the only thing taken seriously is the responsibility at hand.

With this new attitude, where is the tension that existed in past projects?

Did it desert, too?

BEWARE! LAUGHTER AT ONESELF CAN SERIOUSLY DAMAGE ONES POMPOSITY.

The bouyancy of enthusiasm solidifies desire with faith.

The energy in this powerful combination arrives at the goal at an effortless tempo.

Enthusiasm, desire and faith, the divine powers within, are readily available when the acceptance is sincere.

Some obstacles creating a separation from this good are the shadows of fear, doubt and disbelief.

There may be other shadows lurking too, if subconsciously, failure is the goal.

ENTHUSIASM HANDILY OVERCOMES THE OBSTACLES IN OUR PROJECTS.

Faith is a motivator of courage that accomplishes goals even under the most difficult conditions.

It is not measured by either weight or size, but is an undeterred will of acceptance.

Because of its divine nature, the manifestation, at times, is classified a miracle.

On a personal basis, miracles are not unusual for a practitioner of faith.

FAITH.

Worlds washed in negativity lack a foundation of love for happiness to frolic on.

The world of hate is a warped misunderstanding of love.

Jealousy is too insecure to see the truth.

Anger in its confusion is intolerant of life in the happy lane.

Fear hesitates due to lack of faith to thrust forward.

Adhering to these limitations furnishes an illusion of power deluding them as Gods, not realizing their *false nature*.

HATE JEALOUSY ANGER FEAR

DICK JACHIM

WHICH FALSE GOD SHOULD I REFUSE TO ACCEPT TODAY?

Fear of confronting an issue by evading it, can be the beginning of a long, torturous, emotional journey.

Replacing fear which is an illusion without a foundation, with faith which comes from the divine source within, brings along courage to gently, but firmly, confront the issue and resolve it.

The outcome of the solution is secondary, some are better than others.

The confrontation is the *key* to a happy life.

HEAD IN SAND IS NOT CONDUCIVE TO NORMAL BREATHING.

When in an unknown or uncompromising position, fear can be utilized as an ally.

Fear refines alertness to its extreme and increases the energy into a powerful force to confront and neutralize the situation at hand.

This was a discipline understood and practiced in World War II by the Second Armored Division, U.S. Army, and undoubtedly by all the armed forces.

Also, on an individualized basis, atheists do not exist in battle areas.

There may be a useful lesson in spiritual growth from this on a civilian level, as well.

A SHADOW OF THE MIND.

A feeling of inadequacy is fertile thought for the expectancy of defeat, a form of self-inflicted punishment.

This results in a martyr complex appropriately defended with the attitude: "Why me?"

Tired of being a turkey? Then embody a touch of faith and feel the illusion of inadequacy vanish. This exposes a flash of adequacy ready to expand; also igniting the attitude with sparkles of love and happiness in this change.

WHY ME ! !

Forgiveness is a divine action that dissolves condemnation and replaces it with love.

Silently the power of love must fill the space which prevents condemnation from returning to block the channel to happiness.

Without forgiveness, self-crucifixion prevails.

**FORGIVENESS IS A TICKET
TO HAPPINESS.**

Chapter 4

A goal without obstacles is like obstacles without a goal, non-existent.

When focus on the accomplishment can wisely measure the challenge necessary to success, the path becomes more tenable; sometimes even more enjoyable than the end result.

So hang in there, you are probably having more fun than you think at the present.

NO MATTER HOW TOUGH IT SEEMS, HANG IN THERE.

Pleasures received in reaching a goal lie in the sharing of it, the reflection of the pursuit in reaching it, and the glow in the contentment from it.

The crowning honor, however, is the respect success breeds.

The responsibility for these accolades should best be described as modesty, the symbol of a matured stature.

If the ego cannot fit into a pocket, it is over fed and needs to diet.

**A GOAL CAN BE THE SIZE OF A MANSION OR HUT.
SUCCESS, HOWEVER, IS IN THE SIZE OF THE JOY EXPERIENCED DAILY WHILE PURSUING IT.**

A talent developed benefits the world.

It comes in many types of inspirations: Soothing, Joyous, Insightful, to name a few.

This educated energy created by a developed talent permeates the world in its subtle way, adding vibrations of an affirmative nature from which all may benefit, consciously or subconsciously.

It is also a sign of thanksgiving to the Divine Being for bestowing the talent.

IMPROVE YOURSELF AND YOU IMPROVE THE WORLD!

Not allowing the time necessary to perceive events, is inviting limitation to participate in life.

The level of prosperity reached, is the measure of knowledge perceived and practiced.

Ignorance, on the other hand, is the limitation that still exists.

YOU'RE PADDLING YOUR FEET IN MY LIVING ROOM. IGNORANCE IS THE MYSTERY FOUND IN KNOWLEDGE AND COMPREHENSION.

An irritation can be a reminder that remedial action is necessary to manifest a healing.

This successful healing may become an added refinement to life's daily experience.

Therefore, a serious focus on correcting an irritation can become one's shining hour, or a need for a fly swatter.

AN IRRITATION CAN BE THE START OF SOMETHING GOOD.

Jealousy appears when one's stature is toad-high.

To be rid of jealousy, raise the stature to human-size. This is done by a mental adjustment.

Begin with an appearance before a mirror. Next, replace the inferiority complex with the truth, which is, that *you are one of a kind.* Now with this knowledge, it is easy to learn to like yourself to complete the change-over.

Your stature is now HUMAN-SIZE.

Congratulations !

JEALOUSY IS PART OF A TOAD. TRY NOT TO BE A TOAD. STAY A PEOPLE.

Judging critically creates the food which can feed an abundance of misery.

This diet is not conducive to attraction, but very much so to isolation.

Changing the main ingredient to tolerance, sprinkled with a bit of happiness for added flavor, creates a concoction loved by all.

And . . . isolation gives way to attraction.

**TO ATTRACT OTHERS
JUDGE NOT.**

To be judgmental can be a personality failure evolved from chaos.

This superior mental facade can obscure a house full of turmoil from view.

Criticisms are mostly reviews of one's personal collection.

The results can be happy or unhappy experiences.

The happy ones are usually those seen through the mirror.

**TO JUDGE IS TO GET INVOLVED.
AN INVOLVEMENT IS EITHER A
HAPPY OR AN UNHAPPY
EXPERIENCE.**

… Chapter 5

Desire without substance is an imposter. It belongs in the world of illusion, the dream world.

Desire, however, with determination is a power known as faith, which is an invisible presence within.

When awakened to fulfill a goal, faith becomes divinely inspired into a formidable attitude that cannot be deterred.

Obstacles along the path of completion only temper the attitude to the strength of steel. This adds flavor to the manifestation.

OUR WANTS ARE FULFILLED AT THE LEVEL OF ACCEPTANCE.

When confusion, in company with limitation, prevents the manifestation of a solution, anxiety can be the influential factor, with fear probably cheering on.

To resolve this situation, simply and effortlessly, release the present actors and go within thought and hire the assistance of the *Divine Presence*. The fee is very nominal, just for the asking.

Bind this new agreement with faith; then peace of mind prevails, and the solution is waiting to be recognized.

**CONFUSION IS THE CHILD
OF LIMITATION.**

To repair the mental fence of limitation, release the prisoners responsible for the damage to the universal court of law.

Appointing tolerance as the judge and courage as the prosecutor, the prisoners named jealousy, fear or whatever are assured a fair trial.

Sentenced to forgiveness and released to the custody of love and faith, they are assigned to repairing the fence.

Through divine guidance the boards of limitation are replaced with those of prosperity and secured with the sturdy nails of discipline.

And of course, all live happily ever after.

WARPED FENCE OF LIMITATION.

Differences are the individualizations of the whole. Therefore, countries, cultures and personalities are all manifestations from the one, the Supreme Being.

As this realization keeps expanding in consciousness, more lovingness is seen in others, which is the direct reflection of the viewer.

Continuing along this path to the state of illumination, arrival at the destination is the direct contact with reality which, of course, is God.

**LIFE IS A LIMITLESS VARIATION
IN ITS ONENESS WITH ALL.**

For so much meaningful givingness in a relationship, a dog is an excellent portrait of unconditional love.

The nature of this givingness is a blend of words that transform into tolerance as the mode of activity.

Beginning with love, the words in this blend are simple ones. Such as, sincerity, reliability, absoluteness, tolerance, companionship, enthusiasm, faith, joy and happiness.

A complicated word such as forgiveness is unnecessary, for there is nothing to forgive in this blend.

DICK JACHIM

**THIS IS A SYMBOL OF LOVE,
LOYALTY, FORGIVENESS
AND WHOSE TURN IS IT TO
PICK-UP IN THE YARD.**

Love restricted by circumstance is a focus on a personal weakness that usurps happiness.

Replacing the restriction with a touch of humor may be the antidote needed to return love to a healthy position of wholeness.

When the path to growth in consciousness is smooth and sturdy, the depth of love in it is considerable.

If it crackles and cracks from the weight of an opinionated attitude, it just stumbles along.

**LOVE IS LOVING EVEN WHEN
ONE IS NOT CONFORMING.**

Love is the breath of the heart as air is the breath of the body. Both are necessary to sustain life.

The many facets of love, such as beauty, joy and self-givingness to mention a few, are pronounced reflections of God.

When love prevails only the wholeness of the good life exists, for no condemnation can survive.

**LOVE
BEGINS IN THE MIRROR.**

The sensitive colors, the fragile tenderness, and the regal dignity of a flower is a composition of matchless beauty. This could only be the physical side of divine love.

Another sign that this must be true, is that this beautiful, tender and so fragile flower blossoms everywhere, even in desolate areas where the sturdiest of plants are not expected to grow.

Therefore, a pause in one's travels to savor this love from God makes for a happier traveller.

**FLOWERS ARE THE FACE OF A
GARDEN. A GARDEN IS THE
BEAUTY QUEEN OF THE UNIVERSE.**

Love is a force of creation and the sustenance of survival.

Love is multiple in scope. It can be practiced many ways and everywhere.

When in its finest refinement, it is balance expressing itself.

Love's attire is a solemn dignity washed in bright light and accented with ecstasy.

Void of negativity, its appearance is contentment, which is the reflection of God.

LOVE IS EVERYWHERE, SPARKLING IN MANY DIFFERENT FACETS.

The warmth of an embrace is spiritually endowed with love-filled healing properties, physically and emotionally.

It increases the value of life, and lightens the burden with an affirmative attitude.

It is the simplest effort and results in a phenomenal return of healing, for oneself and the world.

**GREETING WITH A HUG
IS EXHILARATING,
AND SO HEALTHY,
AND SO — AND S-O-O-O.**

Chapter 6

Emptiness as space is one of the most valuable elements of survival on this planet.

The characteristics identify the type of space: Like the parking lot, an elevator shaft, a gopher hole, an ocean, or air to name a few.

Meditation is a form of space, too. Some of the things meditation is useful for are: deep thinking, praying, resting mentally, and planning a change of scenery.

Then there is that special space made exclusively for the **doughnut** so that it will never be mistaken for a biscuit.

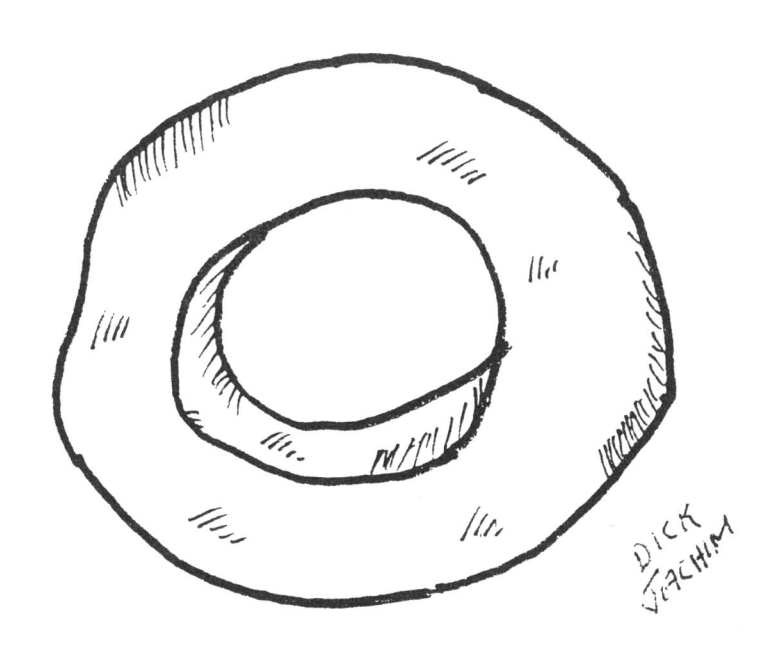

A DOUGHNUT COULD NOT BE A DOUGHNUT WITHOUT THAT SPECIAL EMPTINESS.

The egg is a symbol of the beginning of life.

In ancient Egypt and India, the symbol of the egg plays an important mythical role in the account of the creation of the world.

In the United States of America, the egg's importance is symbolized as the foundation for creating a life-giving breakfast.

Life is recognized at the morning awakening and sustained then by the egg.

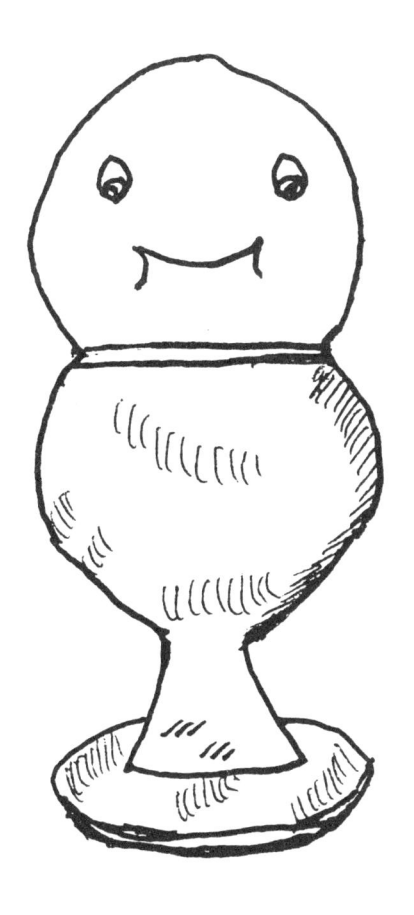

**A GOOD EGG IS ACCEPTED
EITHER FRIED, BOILED
OR HATCHED.
A BAD EGG IS SENT AWAY.**

A smile is a pleasant salutation that is enjoyed and acknowledged by others.

It has a magnetic charm that lightens the burden in the daily routine, as well as in an unknown environment.

A smile is a universal symbol of goodwill.

Many times it is accompanied by a twinkle in the eyes, a sign that happiness exists and a bit of humor is enjoyed.

A smile before breakfast and before dinner gives away the type of day expected and experienced.

A FACE WITH A SMILE IS A SIGN THAT ONE IS NOT ALL BAD.

An unexpected event is only one from a continuous process of events experienced daily.

Many, by their insignificance, do not receive much attention, if any, on the conscious level.

The medium-sized events do get noticed because the experiences are more pronounced with satisfaction or distaste.

Then there is the heavy drama type, which, usually results in a lifeshaking experience, favorable or unfavorable.

These events are never lost, they just keep accumulating and reflecting in the composure of an individual's personality.

That's what life is all about.

COMPOSURE IS TESTED BY THE UNEXPECTED.

A problem is the container enclosing the solution. It is of many designs, overwhelmingly physical in appearance, but is mostly mental.

Being a new experience, it is capable of creating an attitude of formidable power to discourage penetration.

The aura of fear, intrigue, confusion, and many other head-scratching thoughts emanate before the breakthrough to the solution is reached.

The prize for this success can be from a simple to a tremendous feeling of satisfaction. Most important, however, is a gain in stature.

SCIENCE OF MIND TEACHES TO REGARD PROBLEMS AS OPPORTUNITES. ANYONE FOR THIS BOX OF OPPORTUNITIES ?

A seeming mistake may be an unfoldment of a fruitful opportunity through the sixth sense . . . intuition.

Keeping an open mind instead of getting frustrated as to why the error was made, allows the channel to your inner self to stay open for any message.

Therefore, to what may seem a mistake, practice the silence and become attuned to any realization that may be signaled.

**A MISTAKE CAN BECOME
AN UNEXPECTED
OPPORTUNITY.**

Experience can be a lesson for growth in consciousness and direction, as well as in the pursuit of a desired accomplishment.

Using sixth-sense intuition for guidance in the choice of action, success can manifest sooner with less effort, by superseding many unnecessary experiences found in the intellectual well.

Therefore, reflections found in the silence, bring many insights to the fore effortlessly.

**SUCCESS AND FAILURE ARE
ADJUSTMENTS OF LIFE THROUGH
AN EXPERIENCE.**

Chapter 7

Transcending the crisis, nullifies the stress involved.

With the stress omitted, the crisis is disrobed to its bare facts and the illusion of a giant becomes a pip-squeak.

On this level of consciousness, all the resources and energy can now be utilized to resolve the pip-squeak.

In this form of practice, a problem is considered an opportunity to grow in stature.

WHEN RISING ABOVE A CRISIS, IT SEEMS SO TINY.

Good habits are the end result of good thoughts manifested.

Programming them into a way of life, enhances the daily living by refining the benefits gained from this practice.

This also expands the consciousness to a higher level of appreciation of the good things in life.

All this reflects in one's personality.

**GOOD THOUGHTS ARE FLIGHTY
UNTIL DOMESTICATED INTO
HABIT FORM.**

Thoughts become things when given energy.

Discrimination in the choice of thoughts assures manifestations of an affirmative nature.

The evaluation of the type of thoughts being accepted, are reflected in the personality. It is either magnetic or negative.

Thoughts without energy have no substance and melt away. If they were negative, however, fill the space with a happy thought, like floating a balloon into space.

**NEGATIVE THOUGHTS
WITHOUT ENERGY
MELT AWAY.**

The thought is the inner process which offers ideas, decisions, information, and other choices of enlightenment.

It is divinely subtle, though the most powerful tool available, in formulating a pattern of life.

What is accepted in thought rises to the conscious mind and becomes things.

One is, therefore, a bunch of things operating as a unit.

The value of the unit is determined by the happiness generated.

**POVERTY AND RICHES.
BOTH OF THESE ARE
THE OFFSPRING
OF THOUGHT.**

Taking time to do a mental house cleaning, disposes of the debris, of confusion or boredom, that accumulates from the daily routine.

The refreshing, sparkling, airy space again available finds the thoughts lingering for manifestation or those passing through full of vibrancy.

Happiness returns, again, with the chores effortlessly accepted and accomplished.

Cleansing the vessel has best results by daily meditation, prayer or a combination of both, though other choices are available.

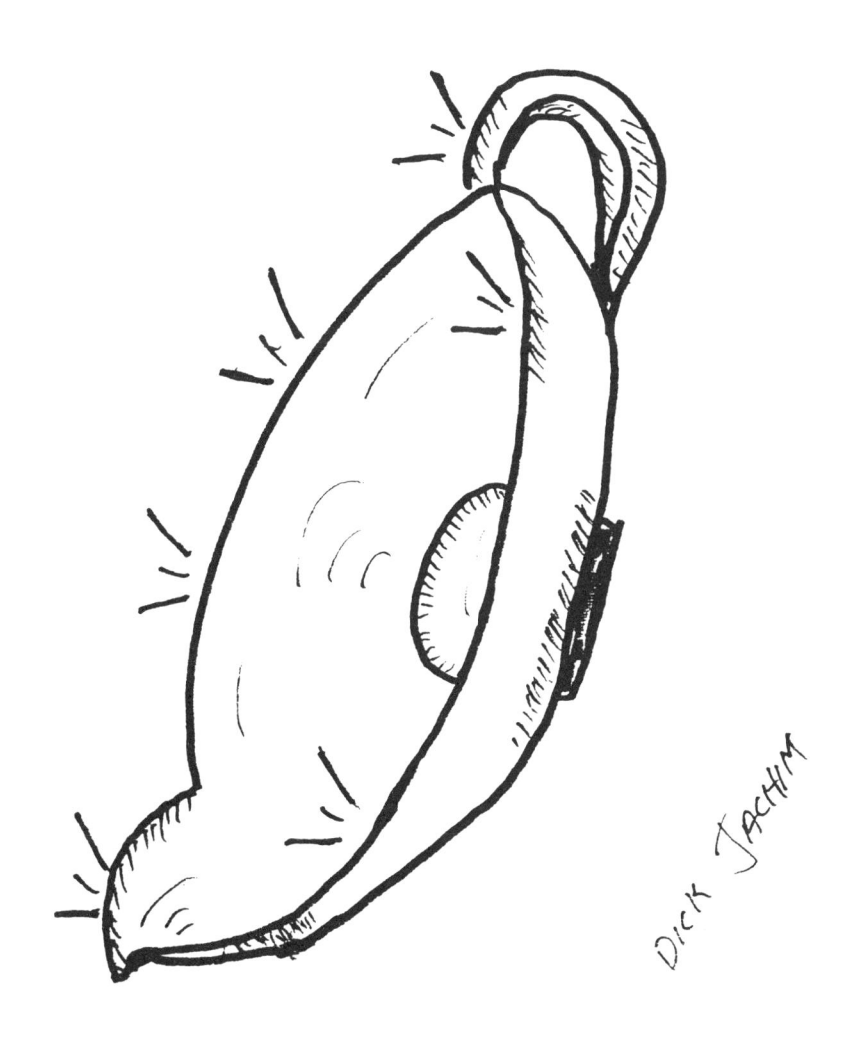

**AWARENESS OF THE BEAUTY
IN THE EMPTINESS
OF THE VESSEL
IS THE KNOWLEDGE THAT
CLEANSING IS NOW COMPLETE.**

An open mind is an open door to allow a flow of ideas to visit.

Some come dressed as daydreams; others as whimsical delights in reverie; and occasionally, one will bring a gift of enhancement by which to prosper.

This gift, when practiced, expands the consciousness to a happier level of life.

All this by leaving the door open.

**WELCOMING IN A NEW IDEA
MAY BE THE BEGINNING OF
A PROSPEROUS RELATIONSHIP.**

An exhilarating atmosphere forms tranquillity because love prevails.

This is accomplished by temporarily separating from the burden of the daily routine into a cherished activity, which no matter how nominal in value, is a luxurious pause.

A pause that is embellished with joy in the anticipation and satisfaction in the change of the activity.

This exhilaration continues, then, into the aftermath by dissolving the burden of the daily routine, as if touched by a magic wand.

TRANQUILLITY IS FISHING WITHOUT BAITING THE HOOK.

The environment in which the daily routine is accepted determines the level of contentment.

At times for some, it can be most satisfying to be outdoors in the rough with all the amenities likewise. For others, a lawn chair in the midst of luxury obtains the same results.

To become disenchanted with the present environment, necessitates a change in thinking . . . from a life of rustic in stature to a degree of luxury or vice versa.

Thinking followed by action is the formula.

CONTENTMENT.

Slavery prevails when thought lacks wisdom, thus creating an undisciplined tongue.

Voicing an opinion to confront a situation that needs correcting, however, can be a sincere act that gains respect and, probably, a *solution*.

An opinion spoken without substance is usually a bid to purchase a consequence flavored distastefully.

"Mum's the word" pays many dividends.

Dick Jachim

MASTER OF THE UNSPOKEN WORD AND SLAVE TO THE SPOKEN.

ORDER FORM

CES PUBLISHING
POST OFFICE BOX 55967
SHERMAN OAKS, CA. 91403

_____ Copies of Reach For The Cookies at $ ~~11.95~~ 9.95 each

NAME _____

ADDRESS _____

_____ ZIP _____

Shipping: $1.00 for first book and $ .25 for each additional book.
Please send check or money order payable to CES Publishing.